Celtic

Geometric
Quilts

Camille Remme

American Quilter's Society
P. O. Box 3290 • Paducah, KY 42002-3290

Located in Paducah, Kentucky, the American Quilter's Society (AQS), is dedicated to promoting the accomplishments of today's quilters. Through its publications and events, AQS strives to honor today's quiltmakers and their work – and inspire future creativity and innovation in quiltmaking.

Editor – Bonnie K. Browning
Book Design – Lanette Ballard
Illustrations – Whitney Hopkins & Lanette Ballard
Cover Design – Karen Chiles

Library of Congress Cataloging-in-Publication Data

Remme, Camille.
    Celtic geometric quilts / by Camille Remme.
          p.   cm.
    Includes bibliographical references (p.).
    ISBN 0-89145-870-0
    1. Patchwork--Patterns. 2. Quilting--Patterns. 3. Decoration and
Ornament, Celtic.   I.   Title.
    TT835.R455 1996
    746.46'041--dc20

                            96-44789
                              CIP

Additional copies of this book may be ordered from: American Quilter's Society, P.O. Box 3290, Paducah, KY 42002-3290 @ $16.95. Add $2.00 for postage & handling.

Printed in the U.S.A. by Image Graphics, Paducah, KY

Contents

INTRODUCTION

People have always been interested in creating family trees and discovering their heritage. The desire to discover our beginnings brings insight into the meaning of our lives.

My interest in Celtic art and mythology has made me more aware of other levels of influence and knowing that create an individual. I realize now that Celtic myth is very much my heritage since my ancestors trace back to the British Isles. This is reflected in my customs, rituals, and religion. Celtic lore may be 3,000 years old but it is also very alive today in symbols such as the Christmas tree, Halloween, mistletoe, the Celtic cross, a reverence for the land, water, and sun. The Grail quest, the power of Excalibur, the magic of Merlin, the harmony of Camelot, the fairness of the knights of King Arthur's Round Table, and many more stories and symbols are imprinted in our unconscious.

My Celtic quest started with unexpected events and experience at first – trip to England, visits to Stonehenge and Bath, a teenage daughter immersed in using the designs, a sister taking me to the play, *Camelot*, and seeing that there were many geometric (straight-edged) Celtic designs. Once I was hooked on creating with Celtic designs, my enthusiasm grew, and I learned what I could about the Celtic people who lived so many centuries ago. In doing so I also learned more about myself.

Each quilt I make and each design I draw, is a new journey because the blocks and designs are filled with underlying meanings. Celtic art is symbolic of ageless, transcendent design.

Camille Remme
Toronto, 1996

4

▶ The instructions and patterns in this book are intended for any level quilter who is familiar with using a rotary cutter, and who has the ability to transfer cut fabric strips into a block based on graph paper designs.

▶ All quilt blocks are drawn on graph paper with 1 square equaling 1".

▶ All detail lines added to the blocks in this book are based on actual Celtic design lines.

▶ Instructions are written for making one block, but always make enough repeat blocks to fit your size quilt for efficiency in the cutting and sewing processes.

▶ No fabric requirements are given for any projects. You will need an adequate fabric stash. All blocks are made from a combination of strips, squares, and triangles.

▶ When making a Celtic quilt, you do not need to preplan the whole design, just have an overview plan in the form of a rough drawing. Staying flexible and moving the repeat blocks around in different design areas allow the unexpected to come forth.

▶ All diagrams show only finished sizes, but the written instructions give the cutting sizes.

SYMBOLISM

▶ Symbols communicate without using language.

▶ A symbol implies nothing is as it first appears.

▶ The symbol has no power; what it represents exerts the influence.

▶ Meaningful symbolism transcends the personality and mind, touching the soul.

▶ The exact meaning of a given symbol is elusive; more important is the path one is guided down and the questions awakened within.

▶ The rise of interest in Celtic and other cultures' symbols points out our need to take an inner journey.

▶ As we become self-actualized through self-realization and self-awareness, the need for symbolism disappears.

Celtic Design for Quilts

What has survived of Celtic art – in stonework, jewelry, and manuscripts – has its own recognizable quality. The art and designs are important because the Celtic people left no written history.

What continues to draw me to the Celtic designs is the way they were used lushly and freely in all areas of a decorated surface. Color was also used boldly and skillfully in the surviving Celtic manuscripts such as the *Book of Kells* and the *Lindisfarne Gospels*. Also of interest is the fact that most of the designs have meanings and messages implied, creating a depth of the design rarely found in other artistic styles.

I was initially drawn to Celtic design because repeating geometric blocks and lively color could be used. Quilts are made by cutting fabric into strips and machine piecing repeat blocks or units to create a pleasing overall design. Many of the designs used, particularly the key and maze blocks, have been very adaptable to this technique. And on further examination, many of the curved knot and border designs could also be redrawn and sewn using the same techniques.

The important key to re-creating Celtic-looking designs was the use of zigzag stitching in black, gold, and silver applied in and around the blocks. In doing this, the lines used by ancient Celtic scribes when writing the *Book of Kells* and the other manuscripts are re-created. The finished quilts feel both old and new in design.

6

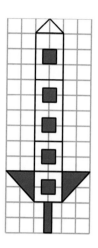

6 x 13

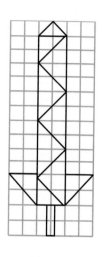

6 x 15

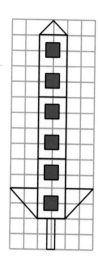

6 x 15

Excalibur was the name of King Arthur's sword. The sword symbolizes power and how its misuse can lead to its loss.

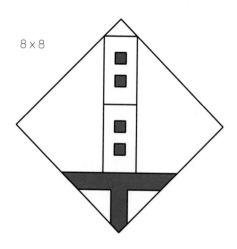

8 x 8

10 x 10 when floated with background strips.

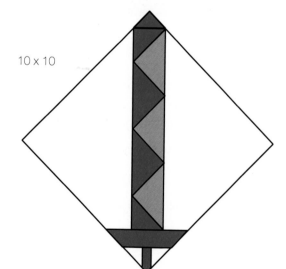

10 x 10

12 x 12 when floated.

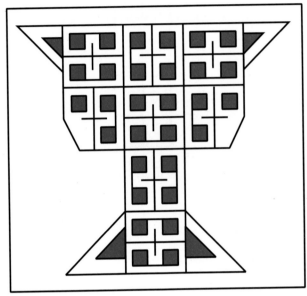

20 x 20

6 x 7

7 x 7

The search for the Grail symbolizes the search for the answers to life. It is implied that all mysteries would be solved if the Grail were discovered. There are other symbols representing the finding of wisdom – eg. the philosopher's stone and the light, but the Grail is a strong Celtic symbol.

15 x 15

❧ The Celtic cross represents the union of heaven and earth. It predates the Christian cross by centuries. This cross has a circle around the crossing axis that symbolizes the sun, the wheel of life, and wholeness.

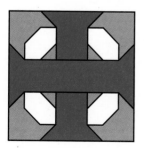

8 x 8

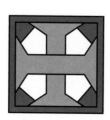

5 x 5

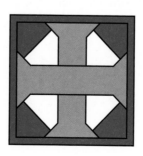

7 x 7

9 x 12

CELTIC TRIPLE ENCLOSURE

10

14" x 14"

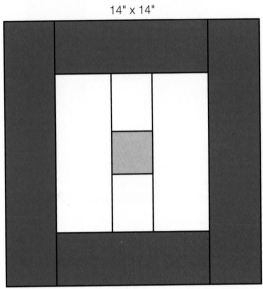

Center
Cut 4½" sq.

Representative of human consciousness, the first square in the center of the Celtic triple enclosure symbolizes the unconscious mind and spirituality. The third square is the reality of the physical world. The second square is the link to both aspects of life.

❦ The unbroken line of the knotwork represents spiritual growth toward eternal life. It is the interlacing path of life.

Endless Knot

❦ The endless knot is a continuous line which represents continuity and eternity. This symbol is also found in Chinese and Hindu art.

MAZE OR SPIRALS

SPIRAL

🌿 Spirals symbolize eternal life. The center of the spiral symbolizes complete balance; it is the point where heaven and earth are joined.

5 x 5

6 x 6

7 x 7

MAZE – KEY PATTERNS

🌿 Maze designs are spirals in straight lines. Key patterns are angular paths which keep separating and rejoining. They are symbolic of seemingly disjointed events in life that come together again to form a stronger, cohesive whole.

Celtic Geometric Quilts

USING COLOR

At first, timid use of color in the Celtic deisgns did not do them justice. The Celtic people were a strong people, and everything about their culture portraying strength and boldness is depicted in their use of color and design. Bright, bold colors, such as Celtic Quest, made in oranges and blues, reflects the boldness. The pages of the *Book of Kells* and other Celtic manuscripts are vibrantly alive through the skillful use of bold colors.

All the Celtic quilts in this book are made of repeat units with two colors in each individual unit. Sewing repeat units in many shades of a color scheme can produce a design with depth, complexity, and a feeling of illumination.

The way to understand the use of color for a single block is to categorize the primary color as the foreground color, and the secondary color as the background or receding color. The primary color should be bright, dark and strong, and warm. The secondary color should be cool with receding intensity. It should be light, but not strong.

For example refer to the quilts Excalibar and The Grail made in yellow and purple. Yellow is used in the foreground and comes forward. Purple used beside yellow will always recede.

VALUE VS. COLOR

Value is a real friend when working with color. Value is the many shades and tones of a color as it expands from light to dark. Regardless of the color family chosen to work with in a quilt, the glow in the design occurs when a wide range of values in that color family is used. For example, in the Celtic Quest quilt many oranges and blues were used. The oranges ranged from peach to reds through rusts. The blues ranged from pastels and medium blues to dark and navy blues with some aqua shades included.

Your fabric stash will dictate how many variations of a repeat block you can set up. Nine to twelve steps of a color family are used in my large quilts. When fabric shopping, always look for new shades or values that will expand the colors in your stash.

We all have favorite colors that pull us to work with them; do not fight this. There are no bad colors, although some are more flexible than others. The real challenge is to expand the chosen color so that it becomes interesting and alive, and to find a contrast to that color that will enliven and enhance it.

When you start a project, lay out an array of fabrics such as the oranges and blues mentioned above that will become the initial palate for a quilt. You may not use all of these shades or you may add to the selection later. Looking at this range of fabrics, you are able to get an overall sense of how the colors will work together. Start by making a smaller Celtic quilt that may need only two or three shades in each color family. Experience is the best teacher to lead into more complex color usage.

13

Construction Notes

▶ Most strips are cut 1½" or 2½".

▶ All triangles are made from squares laid face down on the corners of larger squares or rectangles and sewn diagonally across.

▶ When sewing seam allowances, sew scant ¼" seams. Do not sew exactly on the ¼" line but on the outside of it so the seam allowance is slightly smaller than ¼". When the seams are pressed to one side on the back, the extra allowance gives a more exact block measurement.

▶ To start a quilt, pick an area of design on a rough drawing, and choose a repeat block to fill that space. Many repeat blocks of two colors each can be used. The quilt evolves as the different design areas are positioned against each other.

▶ To create mirror image or reverse blocks, cut all pieces as you would for any block. Make up one sample block and then a reverse block. Use the two blocks as examples for sewing the required number of blocks.

▶ Precision sewing is not mandatory when sewing any of these blocks. The triangle blocks, in particular, always sew up with some variances. Trimming all the blocks to a suggested size will help them fit together easily and neatly during final construction.

▶ To trim up a square block, use a square plastic ruler and place it on top of the block, aligning it with two adjoining edges of the block. Use your rotary cutter to trim up the two edges. Move the ruler to the other two adjoining edges of the block and line the ruler up with the desired measurement lines on the ruler. Cut two straight edges with the rotary cutter.

▶ Floating blocks and borders generally involves sewing 1½" background strips to the trimmed edges of blocks and borders so that the designs appear to float on the background fabric. Many of the continuous cord borders have floating strips added to the two edges after the offset edges are trimmed away.

14

THE BUILDING BLOCKS

The original Celtic blocks designed by scribes flowed easily from one design to another. In this book, I have practiced restraint by making repeat quilt blocks and putting them together in different ways to create a similar effect. Add to this method the potential created by mixing blocks and borders and many new designs become possible.

Some of the designs I have created represent my own concept of the essence of Celtic designs. In some instances, the elements of the Celtic designs have been linked with other primitive design elements, creating a distinctinctive blending of multiple past cultures.

Use this chapter to design your own Celtic quilts. It is an overview of all the blocks used throughout the book.

Also use this chapter when it is time to sew your Celtic finishing lines.

15

Maze Blocks

Sewn Blocks	Celtic Stitching Lines
3 x 3	3 x 3
4 x 4	4 x 4
5 x 5	5 x 5
6 x 6	6 x 6
2 x 4	2 x 4
2½ x 5	2½ x 5
3 x 6	3 x 6

SEWN BLOCKS

5 x 5

6 x 6

5 x 5

6 x 6

7 x 7

7 x 7

CELTIC STITCHING LINES

5 x 5

6 x 6

5 x 5

6 x 6

7 x 7

7 x 7

17

Fretwork Blocks

Sewn Blocks

3 x 3

4 x 4

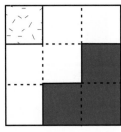

5 x 5

6 x 6

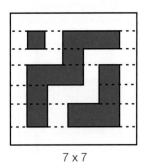

7 x 7

Celtic Stitching Lines

3 x 3

4 x 4

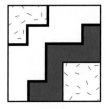

5 x 5

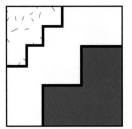

6 x 6

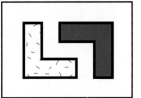

5 x 7

SEWN BLOCKS

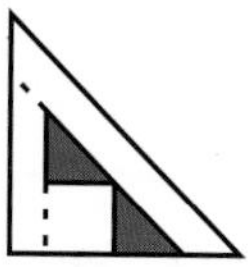

3 x 3

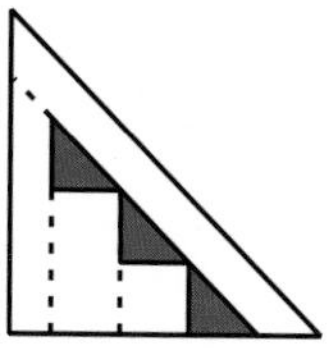

4 x 4

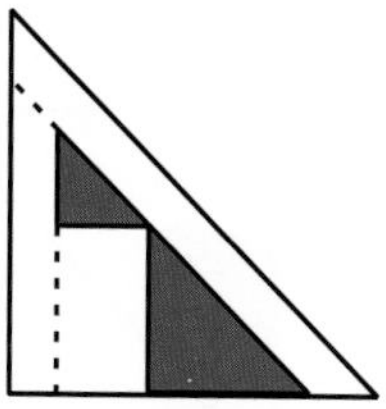

5 x 5

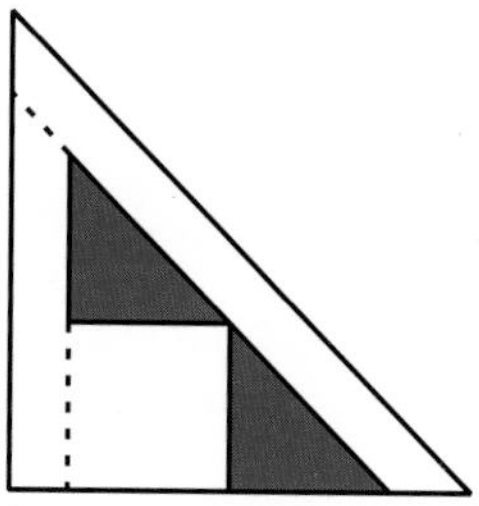

6 x 6

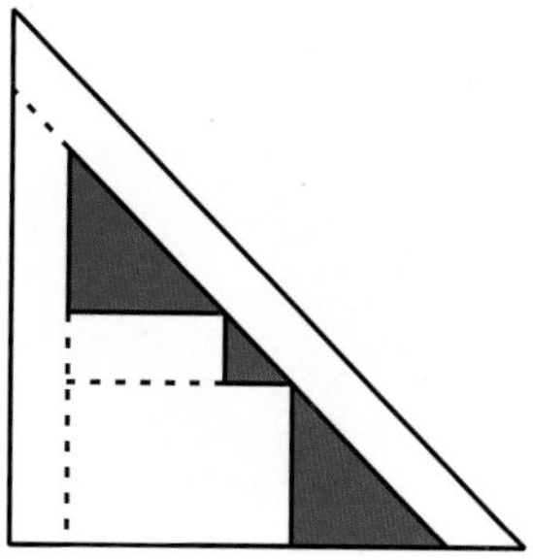

7 x 7

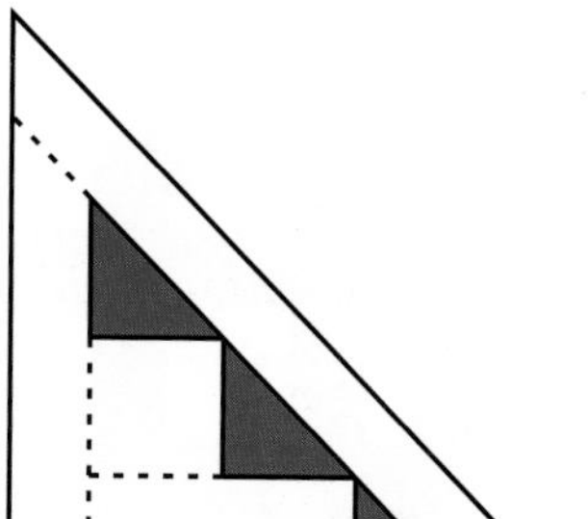

8 x 8

CELTIC STITCHING LINES

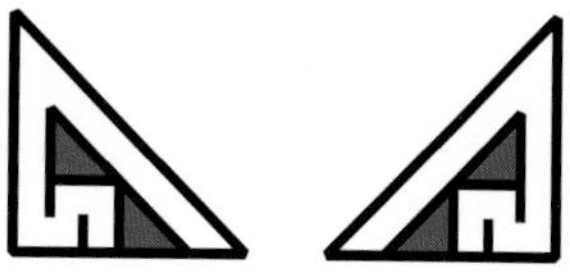

3 x 3

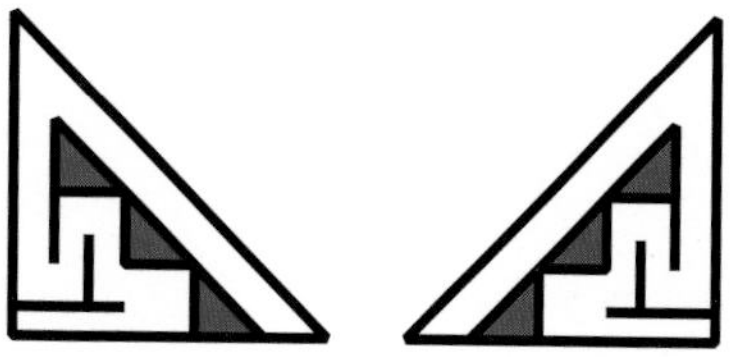

4 x 4

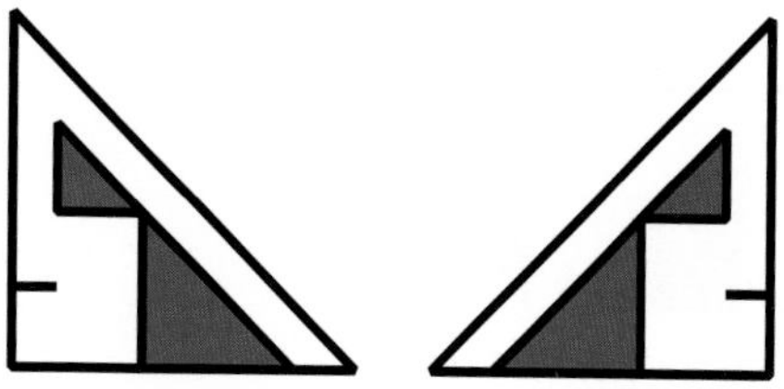

5 x 5

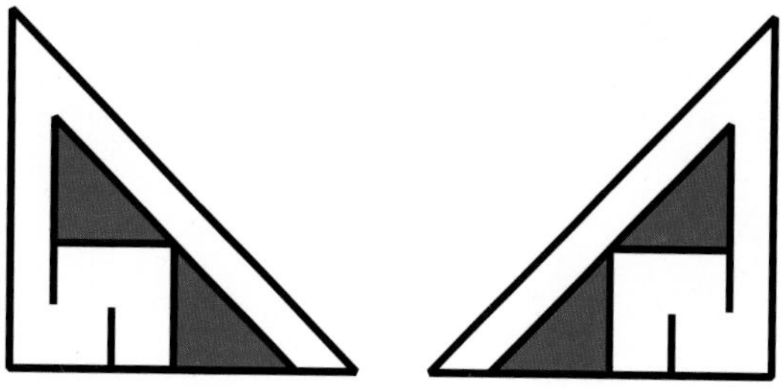

6 x 6

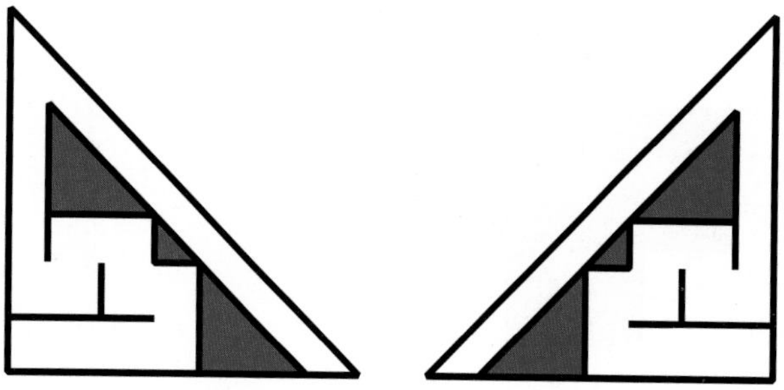

7 x 7

8 x 8

19

Sewn Blocks

Celtic Stitching Lines

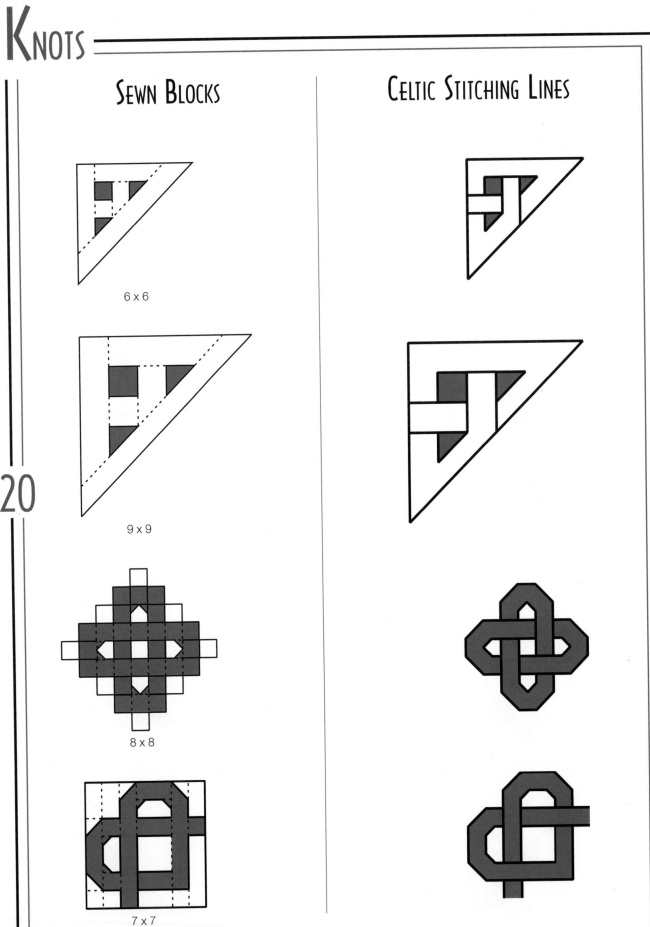

6 x 6

9 x 9

8 x 8

7 x 7

SEWN BLOCKS

4 x 4

4 x 4

5 x 5

7 x 7

5 x 5

5 x 5

CELTIC STITCHING LINES

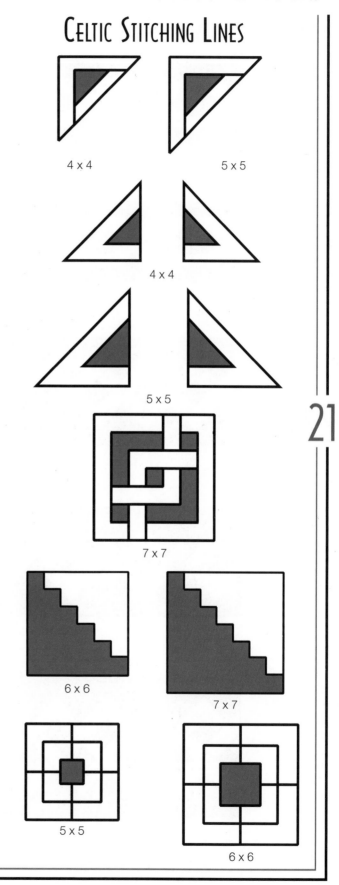

4 x 4

5 x 5

4 x 4

5 x 5

7 x 7

6 x 6

7 x 7

5 x 5

6 x 6

Sewn Blocks

Celtic Stitching Lines

5" wide

5" wide

5½" wide

5½" wide

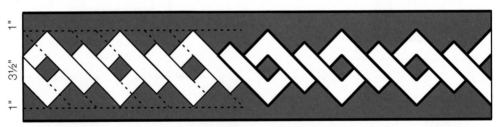

7½" wide

SEWN BLOCKS

CELTIC STITCHING LINES

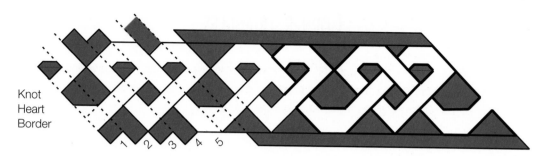

Knot
Heart
Border

Two
Cord
Border

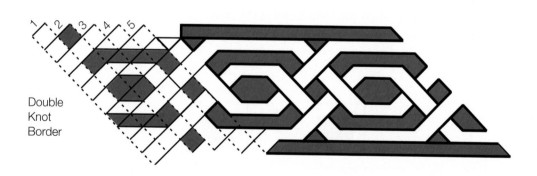

Double
Knot
Border

Large
Geometric
Border

CORNER TRIANGLES

Once you learn the efficient methods for sewing corner triangles, diagonal sewn lines, multiple diagonal lines, trimming the blocks, and floating blocks and borders, you'll be able to create the designs shown and your own variations.

Squares are used to create triangles. Triangles create a more rounded look.

Example:
▶ Cut a background square 1½".
▶ Cut a foreground square 1".

 1½ "
 1"

24

Place the small square on top of the large square, right sides facing. Sew diagonally from corner to corner of the small square. Press the created triangle to the outer edge and trim away middle layer.*

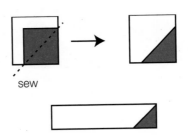

sew

*Do not cut the background square because it is cut the accurate size. The final sewing flows smoother if you are sewing together only accurately cut squares.

DIAGONAL SEWN LINES

This is an efficient way of creating a diagonal line.

Example:
1½" x 2½"

▶ Cut 1½" x 2½" pieces in two colors.
▶ Place one piece on top of the other, right sides together, at right angles, and sew diagonally. Flip the top piece up.

*Note: Two variations are possible. Follow a diagram so that the correct diagonal line is sewn.

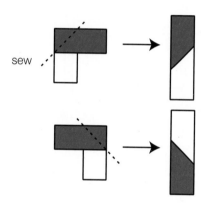

MULTIPLE DIAGONAL LINES

See the Double Knot border (pg. 23).
▶ Create two diagonally sewn pieces as shown. Place one diagonally sewn piece right sides together with two edges aligned and sew as shown.

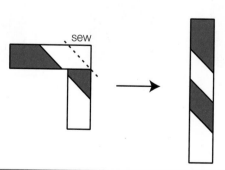

Trimming up the Blocks

Precision sewing is not mandatory when sewing any of these blocks. The triangle blocks, in particular, always sew up with some variances between them. Trimming all the blocks up to a suggested size means that they will all fit together easily and neatly during the final quilt construction.

To trim up a square block use a square plastic ruler and place it on top of the block, aligning it with two edges of the block. Cut two straight edges with a rotary cutter. Move the ruler edges to the other two edges of the block. Line up the two previously cut edges with the desired measurement lines on the ruler and cut two straight edges with a rotary cutter.

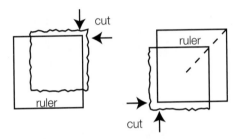

Floating Blocks and Borders

Floating blocks and borders means sewing background fabric strips (usually cut 1½" wide) onto trimmed edges of blocks and borders so that the designs appear to float on the background fabric. Many of the continuous cord borders have floating strips added to the two edges after the offset edges are trimmed away. Any size background strip could be used for floating strips on the sides.

  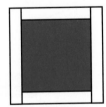

Trimmed block   Sew cut strips on two sides.   Sew cut strips on last two sides.

FOR ONE BLOCK

Finished Block	5" x 5"
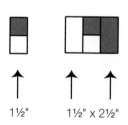 cut 1	1½" sq.
cut 1	1½" x 2½"
cut 1	1½" x 3½"
cut 1	1½" x 3½"

Finished Block	5" x 5"
cut 1	1½" sq.
cut 1	1½" x 2½"
cut 1	1½" x 3½"
cut 1	1½" x 3½"

Sewing sequence:

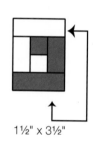 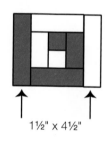 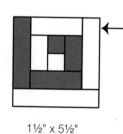

| 1½" | 1½" x 2½" | 1½" x 3½" | 1½" x 4½" | 1½" x 5½" |

By adding a 1½" x 5½" strip to one side, you will have a square block. See four variations below. By reversing the first two squares, you can make two mirror image variations.

Var 1: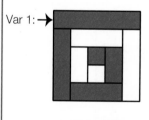

1½" x 5½"
color 2

Var 2: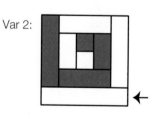

1½" x 5½"
color 1

Var 3: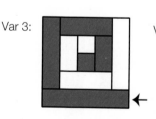

mirror image of Var. 1

Var 4: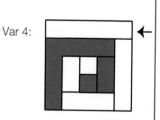

mirror image of Var. 2

27

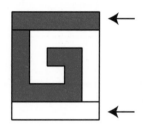

6" x 6"

FOR ONE BLOCK

To create a 6" x 6" block, follow the instructions
for 5" x 5" block to step shown.

▶ Cut a 1½" x 5½" piece from each strip.
▶ Sew onto opposite sides.

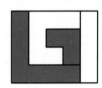

▶ Cut a 1½" x 6½" piece of one of the strips.
▶ Sew onto one side only to create a square block.

You will have a square block with four possible variations, as shown.

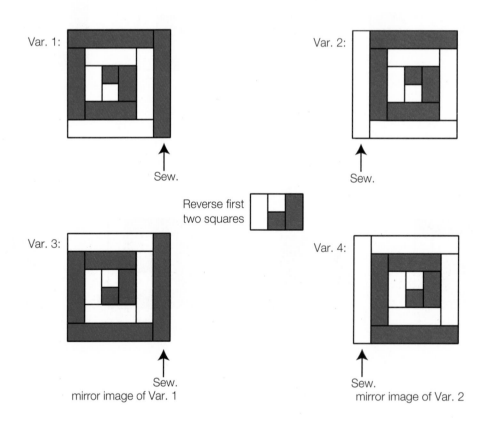

Var. 1:

Sew.

Var. 2:

Sew.

Reverse first
two squares

Var. 3:

Sew.
mirror image of Var. 1

Var. 4:

Sew.
mirror image of Var. 2

Directions for several different mazes are given.

FOR ONE BLOCK

Finished Block		2" x 4"	2½" x 5"	3" x 6"
■ cut 2		1½" sq.	1½" sq.	2" sq.
□ cut 1		1½" sq.	1½" sq.	2" sq.
▭ cut 2		1" x 1½"	1½" sq.	1¼" x 2"
▭ cut 2		1" x 4½"	1¼" x 5½"	1¼" x 6½"
Trim Block to:		2½" x 4½"	3" x 5½"	3½" x 6½"

Sew in sections:

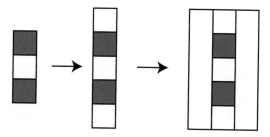

Celtic stitching lines:

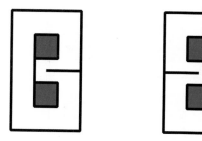

FOR ONE BLOCK

Finished Block		3" x 3"	4" x 4"	5" x 5"	6" x 6"
■ cut 2		2" sq.	2½" sq.	2¾"	3½"
■ cut 1		2½" sq.	3" sq.	3½"	4½"
▬ cut 2		1" x 2½"	1¼" x 3" sq.	1½" x 3½"	1½" x 4½"
▬▬ cut 2		1" x 3½"	1¼" x 4½"	1½" x 5½"	1½" x 6½"
Trim Block to:		3½" sq.	4½"	5½"	6½"

30

Sew in sections:

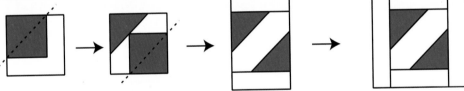

Celtic stitching lines:

To make in reverse change stitch placement.

4-Block Combinations:

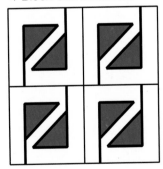

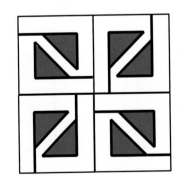

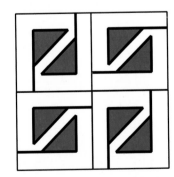

2 blocks & 2 reverse blocks

FOR ONE BLOCK

Finished Block	5" sq.	6"sq.
cut 2	1½" x 2½"	2" x 3½"
cut 2	1½" sq.	1½" x 2"
cut 3	1½" x 3½"	1½" x 4½"
cut 2	1½" x 5½"	1½" x 6½"
Trim Block to:	**5½" sq.**	**6½" sq.**

Sew in sections:

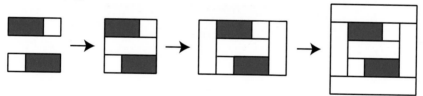

To make in reverse:

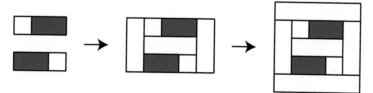

4-Block Combinations, more are possible:

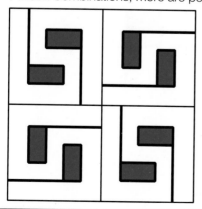
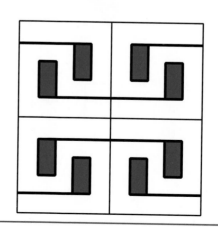

Fret Block Construction

4" x 4"

FOR ONE BLOCK

Finished Block	4" x 4"
cut 1	1½" sq.
cut 1	1½" x 2½"
cut 1	1½" sq.
cut 1	1½" x 2½"
cut 2	1½" sq.
cut 2	2½" sq.
Trim Block to:	4½" x 4½"

Sew:

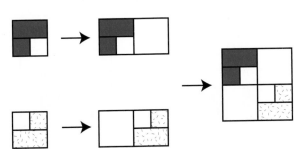

4" x 4"

FOR ONE BLOCK

Finished Block	4" x 4"
cut 2	1½" sq.
cut 1	2½" sq.
cut 1	3" sq.
cut 1	3" sq.
cut 2	1½" sq.
cut 2	1½" x 2½"
Trim Block to:	**4½" x 4½"**

Sew:

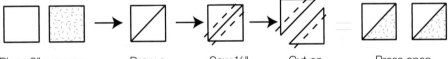

Place 3" squares together, right sides facing.

Draw a diagonal line.

Sew ¼" seams on each side of line.

Cut on diagonal line.

Press open. Trim to 2½" square. Use one per block.

Sew block:

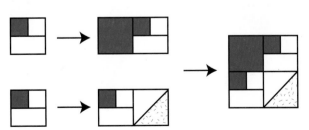

See top of page for added Celtic stitching lines.

FOR ONE BLOCK

Instructions are provided for making four different variations of Key blocks.

Finished Block	4" x 4"	6" x 6"
cut 1 on diagonal	2"	3"
cut 1	1½" sq.	2½" sq.
cut 1	1" x 4"	1½" x 6"
cut 1	1" x 6"	1½" x 10"
Trim Block to:	**5" x 5"**	**7¼" x 7¼"**

34

Sew:

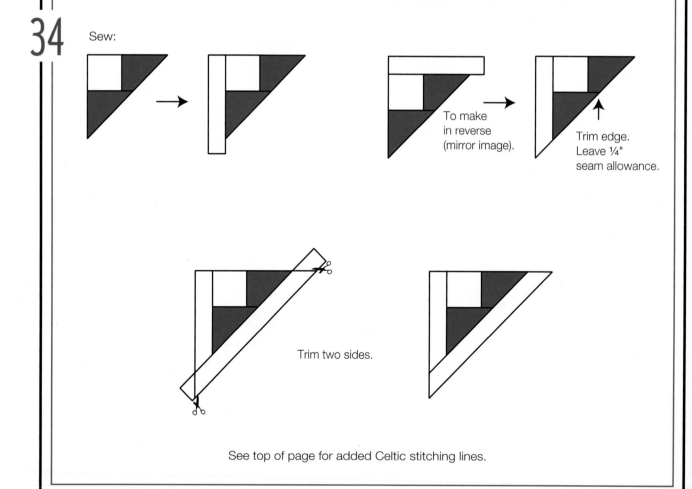

To make in reverse (mirror image).

Trim edge. Leave ¼" seam allowance.

Trim two sides.

See top of page for added Celtic stitching lines.

5" x 5"

FOR ONE BLOCK

Finished Block	5" x 5"
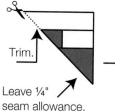 cut 1 on diagonal	2" sq.
cut 1 on diagonal	3" sq.
cut 1	1½" x 2½"
cut 1	1½" x 5½"
cut 1	1½" x 8"
Trim Block to:	**6¼" x 6¼"**

35

Sew:

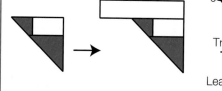

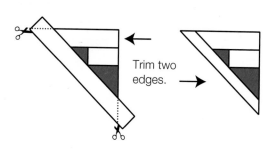

Trim.

Leave ¼"
seam allowance.

Trim two
edges.

To make in reverse

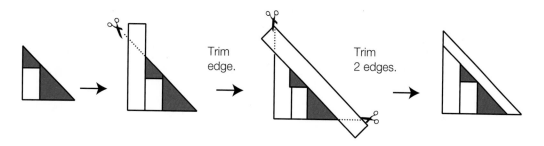

Trim
edge.

Trim
2 edges.

See top of page for added Celtic stitching lines.

Key Block Construction

7" x 7"

FOR ONE BLOCK

From a 1½" strip and a 2½" strip, cut the following:

Finished Block	7" x 7"
cut 1	1½" x 2½"
cut 1	1½" x 7"
cut 1	1½" x 11"
cut 1	2½" x 3½"
cut 1 on diagonal	2" sq.
cut 1 on diagonal	3" sq.

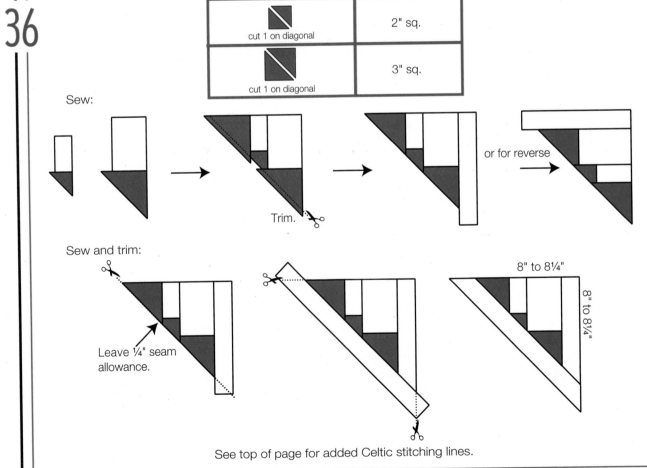

Sew:

Trim.

or for reverse

Sew and trim:

Leave ¼" seam allowance.

8" to 8¼"

8" to 8¼"

See top of page for added Celtic stitching lines.

8" x 8"

FOR ONE BLOCK

Finished Block	8" x 8"
Cut on diagonal. 3 needed.	3" sq.
cut 1	2½" sq.
cut 1	2½" x 4½"
cut 1	1½" x 8"
cut 1	1½" x 14"
Trim Block to:	**9¼" x 9¼"**

Sew:

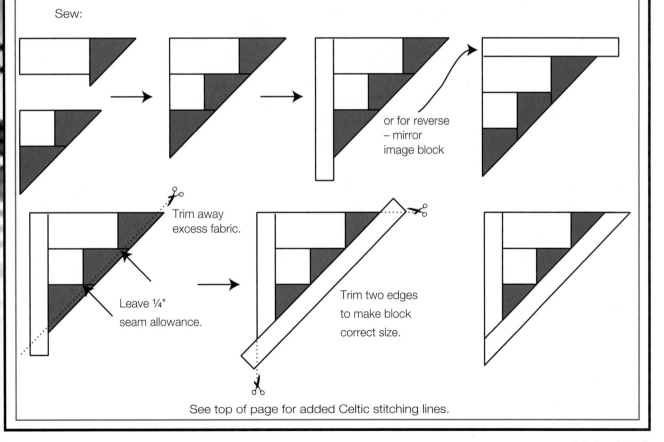

or for reverse
– mirror
image block

Trim away
excess fabric.

Leave ¼"
seam allowance.

Trim two edges
to make block
correct size.

See top of page for added Celtic stitching lines.

Sewing Knot and Cord Blocks

🌱 One of the most important aspects of sewing knot and cord blocks is the Celtic stitching lines which create the illusion of one continuous cord weaving over and under itself.

Note: Floating blocks in background fabric are optional.

FOR ONE BLOCK

Finished Block	4" x 4"	6" x 6"	9" x 9"
■ cut 1	1½" sq.	1½" sq.	2" sq.
⬛ cut on diagonal	2" sq.	2" sq.	2½" sq.
☐ cut 1	1" x 1½"	1½" sq.	2" sq.
▭ cut 1	1" x 2"	1½" x 2½"	2" x 3½"
▭ cut 1	1" x 4"	1½" x 5"	2" x 7"
▭ cut 1	1" x 5"	1½" x 6"	2" x 9"
▭ cut 1	1" x 7"	1½" x 10"	2" x 14"
Trim Block to:	5" x 5"	7¼" x 7¼"	10¼" x 10¼"

Sew:

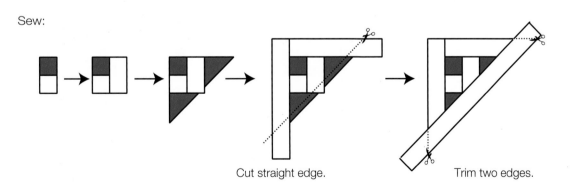

Cut straight edge.   Trim two edges.

See top of page for added Celtic stitching lines.

Continuous Knot Panels

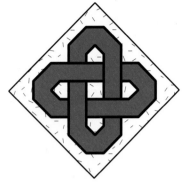

8" x 8" floated

FOR ONE BLOCK

Finished Block:	6" x 6"
cut 4	1" sq.
cut 9	1½" sq.
cut 8	1" sq.
cut 8	1½" sq.
cut 2	1½" x 3½"
cut 2	1½" x 7"
Trim Block to:	6½" x 6½"

Note: Corner triangles are made using two 1" dark squares sewn onto one 1½" light square.

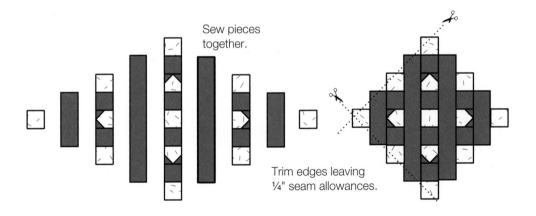

Sew pieces together.

Trim edges leaving ¼" seam allowances.

See top of page for added Celtic stitching lines.

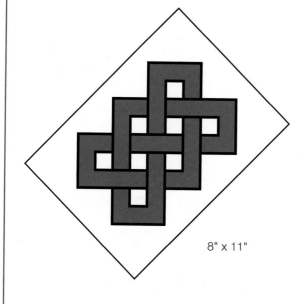

8" x 11"

FOR ONE BLOCK

Finished Block	8" x 11"
cut 8	1½" sq.
cut 5 squares on the diagonal	3" sq.
cut 12	1½" sq.
cut 2	1½" x 3½"
cut 2	1½" x 7½"
cut 1	1½" x 9½"
Trim Panel to:	**8½" 11½"**

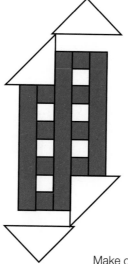

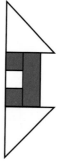

Note: If made with cut 2½" strips, panels would be larger.

Make one and one reverse.

Make one unit.

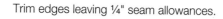

Trim edges leaving ¼" seam allowances.

See top of page for added Celtic stitching lines.

Woven Cord Construction

7" x 7"

FOR ONE BLOCK

Finished Block	7" x 7"
■ cut 3	1½" sq.
■ cut 2	1½" x 2½"
■ cut 2	1½" x 3½"
□ cut 6	1½" sq.
□ cut 3	1½" x 3½"
□ cut 2	1½" x 5½"
□ cut 2	1½" x 7½"
Trim Block to:	**7½" x 7½"**

14" x 14"
Use diagram to apply Celtic stitching lines.

Four blocks make a continuous cord repeat block.

Sew:

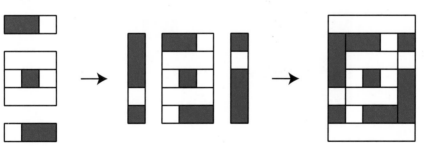

See top of page for added Celtic stitching lines.

17" x 17"

Finished Repeat Large Block 17" x 17"	
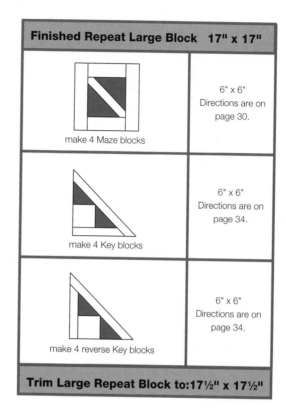 make 4 Maze blocks	6" x 6" Directions are on page 30.
make 4 Key blocks	6" x 6" Directions are on page 34.
make 4 reverse Key blocks	6" x 6" Directions are on page 34.
Trim Large Repeat Block to:17½" x 17½"	

Quilt designs

Repeat block nine or more times.

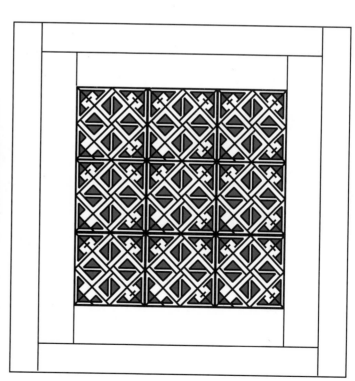

Add two or four borders.

GRAIL BLOCKS

6" x 7"

 The Celtic symbols may appear complex, but are easliy constructed.

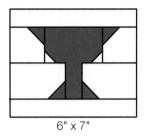

6" x 7"

Sew:

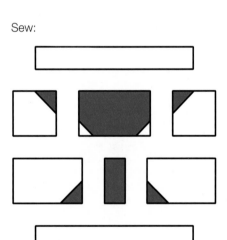

Finished Block	6" x 7"
cut 2	1½" x 7½"
cut 2 for corners	1" sq.
cut 1	2½" x 3½"
cut 2	2½" sq.
cut 4 for corners	1½" sq.
cut 2	2½" x 3½"
cut 1	1½" x 2½"
Trim Block to:	**6½" x 7½"**

7" x 7"

Finished Block	7" x 7"
cut 2	1½" x 7½"
cut 1	3½" sq.
cut 4	2½" x 3½" sq.
cut 4 for corners	1½" sq.
cut 1	1½" x 2½"
cut 2 for corners	1" sq.
Trim Block to:	**7½" x 7½"**

Sew:

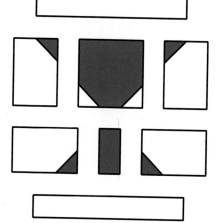

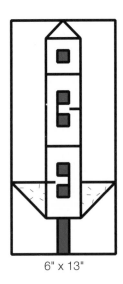

6" x 13"

Sew:

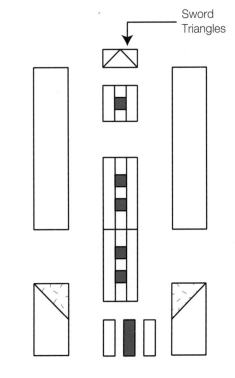

Sword
Triangles

EXCALIBUR

Finished Size	6" x 13"
cut 1	1½" x 2½"
cut 2	1½" sq.
cut 1	1½" sq.
cut 2	1½" sq.
cut 2	1" x 3½"
make 2 maze blocks	2" x 4" Directions are on page 29.
cut 2	2½" x 9½"
cut 2	2½" x 4½"
cut 2	2½" sq.
cut 2	1" x 2½"
cut 1	1½" x 2½"
Trim Block to:	**6½" x 13½"**

46

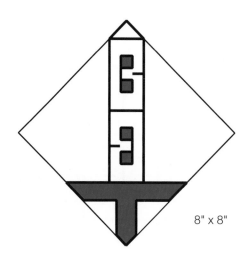

8" x 8"

Excalibur set on point

Finished Block		8" x 8"
 cut 1 on diagonal		8" sq.
 cut 1		2½" sq.
 cut 2 maze blocks		2" x 4" Directions are on page 29.
 cut 1		1½" x 6½"
 cut 1		1½" x 2½"
 cut 1 on diagonal		3" sq.
Trim Block to:		**8½" x 8½"**

Sew:

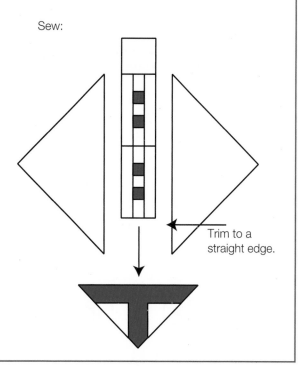

Trim to a
straight edge.

47

5"x 5"

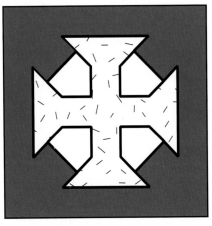

7" x 7"

Finished Block	5" x 5"
cut 2	1½" x 2½"
cut 4	2½" sq.
cut 4	2½" sq.
cut 8 for corners	1½" sq.
cut 1	1½" x 5½"
Trim Block to:	**5½" x 5½"**
To add border:	**7" x 7"**
cut 2	1½" x 5½"
cut 2	1½" x 7½"
Trim Block to:	**7½" x 7½"**

Sew:

  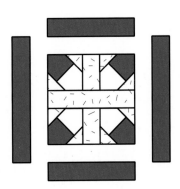

Finished Size	13" x 13"
cut 4	2½" x 5½"
cut 8 for corners	1½" sq.
cut 4	2½" x 3½"
cut 4	3½" sq.
cut 4 for corners	2½"
cut 2	3½" x 5½"
cut 1	3½" x 13½"
Trim Block to:	**13½" x 13½"**
To add border:	**15" x 15"**
cut 2	1½" x 13½"
cut 2	1½" x 15½"
Trim Block to:	**15½" x 15½"**

Make 4

*

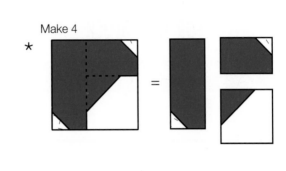

Sew:

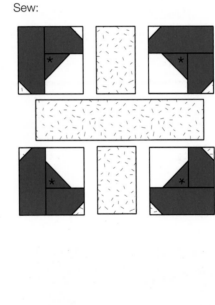

49

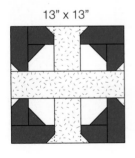

13" x 13"

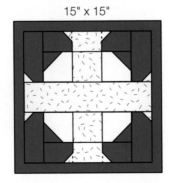

15" x 15"

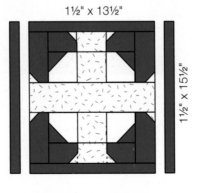

1½" x 13½"

1½" x 15½"

CELTIC TRIPLE ENCLOSURE

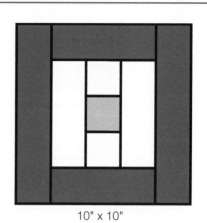

10" x 10"

FOR ONE BLOCK

Finished Block	10" x 10"
■ cut 1	2½" sq.
□ cut 2	2½" sq.
▭ cut 2	2½" x 6½"
▬ cut 2	2½" x 6½"
▬ cut 2	2½" x 10½"

Sew:

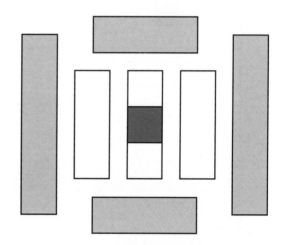

Vary Sizes:

11" x 11"

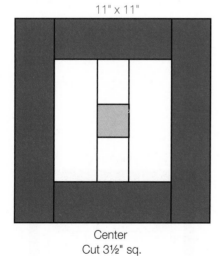

Center
Cut 3½" sq.

14" x 14"

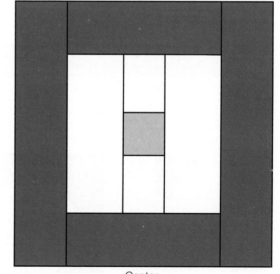

Center
Cut 4½" sq.

50

These intricate looking borders are created by joining two or more pieced strips in an offset pattern. Sometimes there are points to match when sewing the strips; in others, there are no matching points. It is important to check the front side of the strips regularly to see that the correct match-ups are occurring.

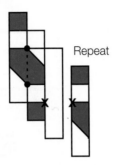

Repeat

If you want to draw up your own version of a continuous cord pattern, or adapt one, sketch it on graph paper. The cord should always weave over and then under. You will know something is wrong if this pattern is not consistent. It is this weaving of the cords that creates a depth to the designs which makes them fascinating.

Instructions are provided on the following pages for several simple Celtic borders, a knot heart border, double knot border, two cord border, geometric border, two maze borders, and a key border.

Sew:

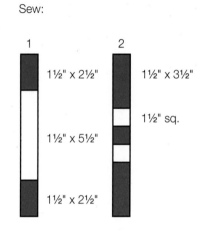

1 1½" x 2½"

1½" x 5½"

1½" x 2½"

2 1½" x 3½"

1½" sq.

Strip 1	
cut 2	1½" x 2½"
cut 1	1½" x 5½"
Strip 2	
cut 2	1½" x 3½"
cut 2	1½" sq.
cut 1	1½" sq.
Trim Strip to:	1½" x 9½"

Repeat strips 1 and 2 (1-2-1-2) to make 5½" wide border (includes background on edges).

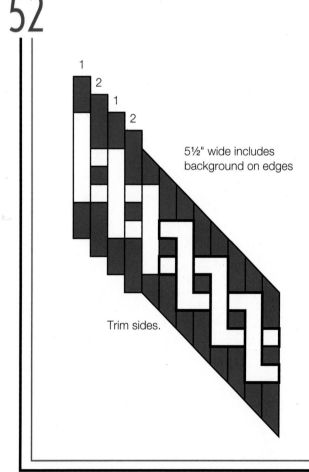

1
2
1
2

5½" wide includes background on edges

Trim sides.

Strip 1	
cut 1	1½" x 3½"
cut 2	1½" x 4½"
cut 1	1½" x 2½"
Strip 2	
cut 2	1½" x 3½"
cut 2	1½" sq.
cut 2	1½" sq.
Trim Strip to:	1½" x 9½"

Repeat strips 1-2-1R to make border. Sew twice as many #1 strips.

Sew:

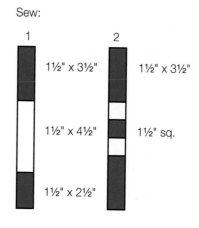

1		2	
	1½" x 3½"		1½" x 3½"
	1½" x 4½"		1½" sq.
	1½" x 2½"		

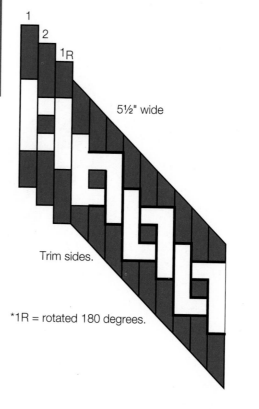

5½" wide

Trim sides.

*1R = rotated 180 degrees.

Sew pieces 1 and 2.
Sew twice as many #2 pieces.

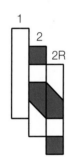

Strip 1	
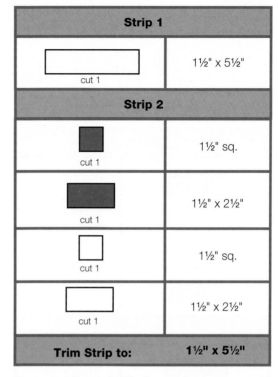 cut 1	1½" x 5½"
Strip 2	
cut 1	1½" sq.
cut 1	1½" x 2½"
cut 1	1½" sq.
cut 1	1½" x 2½"
Trim Strip to:	**1½" x 5½"**

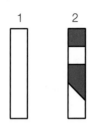

Repeat strips 1-2-2R. Sew twice as many #2 strips. Trim sides leaving ¼" seam allowances. Border is 3" wide; adding 1½" cut strips will make a 5" wide border.

*R = rotate 180 degrees.

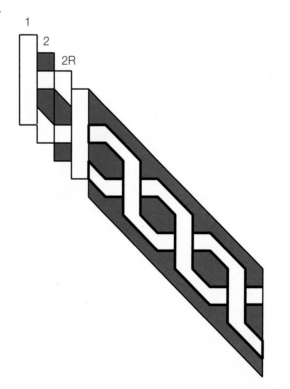

Strip 1	
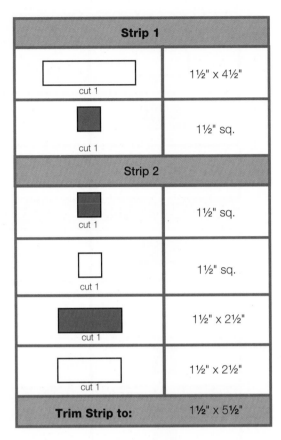 cut 1	1½" x 4½"
cut 1	1½" sq.
Strip 2	
cut 1	1½" sq.
cut 1	1½" sq.
cut 1	1½" x 2½"
cut 1	1½" x 2½"
Trim Strip to:	1½" x 5½"

Repeat strips 1-2-2R. Trim sides leaving ¼" seam allowances. Border is 3" wide; adding 1½" cut strips will make a 5" wide border.

Sew pieces 1 and 2:

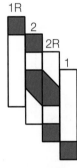

*R = rotate 180 degrees.

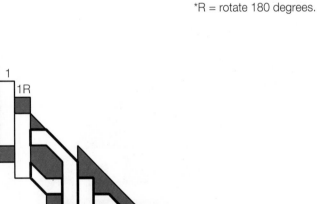

DOUBLE HEART BORDER

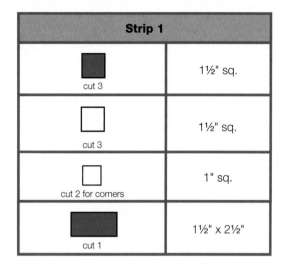

Strip 1	
■ cut 3	1½" sq.
☐ cut 3	1½" sq.
☐ cut 2 for corners	1" sq.
▬ cut 1	1½" x 2½"

Strip 2	
▭ cut 1	1½" x 3½"
▬ cut 2	1½" x 2½"
☐ cut 1	1½" sq.

Strip 3	
▬ cut 1	1½" x 2½"
▭ cut 1	1½" x 5½"
■	1½" sq.

Strip 4	
■ cut 3	1½" sq.
☐ cut 3	1½" sq.
☐ cut 1	1" sq.
▬ cut 1	1½" x 2½"

Strip 5	
▭ cut 1	1½" x 8½"
Trim Strips to:	1½" x 8½"

1 repeat
of pattern

5" wide
7" wide with
floating strips

1
2
3
4
5

Repeat strips 1-2-3-4-5 to make border. Trim edges leaving a ¼" seam allowance.

Border is 5" wide; adding 1½" cut strips on both sides makes a 7" wide border.

Strip 1	
cut 1	1½" x 7½"
cut 1	1½" x 2½"
cut 1	1½" x 2½"

Strip 2	
cut 2	1½" sq.
cut 2	1½" sq.
cut 2	1½" x 2½"
cut 2	1½" x 2½"

Strip 3	
cut 1	1½" sq.
cut 2	1½" sq.
cut 2	1½" x 2½"
cut 2	1½" x 2½"
Trim Strips to:	1½" x 9½"

Repeat strips 1-2-2R-1R-3 to make border. Trim edges leaving ¼" seam allowance.

Border is 5½" wide; adding 1½" cut strips to sides makes a 7½" wide border.

Two Cord Border

Sew:

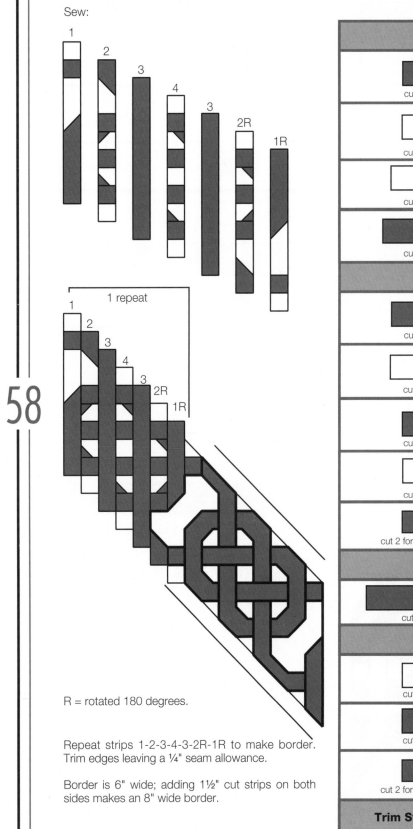

R = rotated 180 degrees.

Repeat strips 1-2-3-4-3-2R-1R to make border. Trim edges leaving a ¼" seam allowance.

Border is 6" wide; adding 1½" cut strips on both sides makes an 8" wide border.

Strip 1	
cut 1	1½" sq.
cut 1	1½" sq.
cut 1	1½" x 3½"
cut 1	1½" x 5½"

Strip 2	
cut 1	1½" x 2½"
cut 1	1½" x 2½"
cut 3	1½" sq.
cut 3	1½" sq.
cut 2 for corners	1" sq.

Strip 3	
cut 3	1½" x 9½"

Strip 4	
cut 5	1½" sq.
cut 4	1½" sq.
cut 2 for corners	1" sq.

Trim Strips to:	1½" x 9½"

Strip 1		
cut 2		1½" x 3½"
cut 3		1½" sq.
cut 2		1½" sq.
Strip 2		
cut 2		1½" x 2½"
cut 1		1½" x 7½"
Trim Strips to:		1½" x 9½"

Repeat strips 1-2 to make border. Trim sides leaving a ¼" seam allowance.

Border is 7" wide.

Sew:

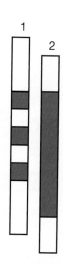

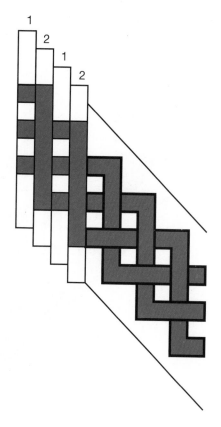

Geometric Border

Variation 1: 2 Fabrics

Variation 1
2 Fabrics

☐ Knots
■ Background

1 2

1R

+   +

Repeat.

Strip 1	
cut 4	1½" x 2½"
cut 1	2½" sq.
cut 2	1½" sq.
cut 2	1½" sq.
Strip 2	
cut 1	1½" x 11½"
Triangles	
cut 2 on diagonal	3½" sq.

1 repeat

Border is 8½" wide

Sew twice as many #1 strips. Sew one triangle to bottom of strip #1 and top of strip #1R; assemble strips #1 and #2.

Stitch triangles to top of strip #1 and bottom of strip #1R to complete one repeat. Trim side edges leaving a ¼" seam allowance.

Variation 2 : 4 fabrics unit 1

Strip 1	
cut 1	1½" x 2½"
cut 1	2½" sq.
cut 2	1½" x 2½"
cut 3	1½" sq.
cut 2	1½" sq.
cut 1	1½" sq.

Strip 2	
cut 2	1½" x 5½"
cut 1	1½" sq.

Strip 3	
cut 2	1½" x 2½"
cut 3	1½" sq.
cut 2	1½" sq.
cut 1	1½" sq.
cut 1	2½" sq.

Triangles	
cut 2 on diagonal	3½" sq.

Variation 2: 4 fabrics.
Unit 1:

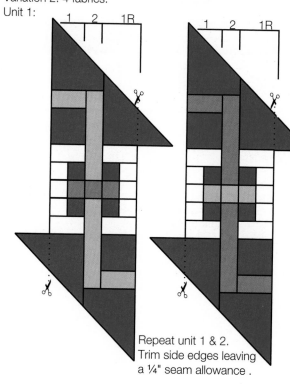

Repeat unit 1 & 2.
Trim side edges leaving
a ¼" seam allowance .

Geometric Border

Variation 2 : 4 fabrics unit 2

Strip 1	
cut 1	1½" x 2½"
cut 1	2½" sq.
cut 2	1½" x 2½"
cut 3	1½" sq.
cut 2	1½" sq.
cut 1	1½" sq.

Strip 2	
cut 2	1½" x 5½"
cut 1	1½" sq.

Strip 3	
cut 2	1½" x 2½"
cut 2	1½" sq.
cut 1	1½" sq.
cut 1	2½" sq.
cut 1	1½" x 2½"

Triangles	
cut 2 on diagonal	3½" sq.

Sew one triangle to the bottom of strip #1; stitch to strip #2. Sew another triangle to the top of this section.

Sew a triangle to the top of strip #3 and add to the strips #1 and 2 section. Sew the fourth triangle across the bottom of strips #2 and #3.

62

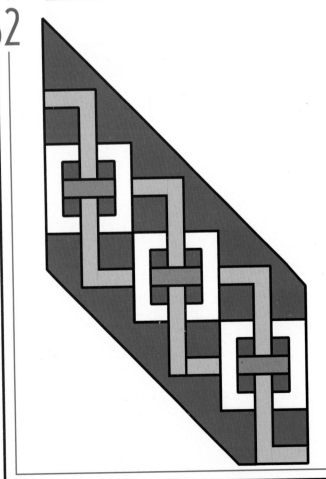

FOR ONE REPEAT

Finished Size	6" wide
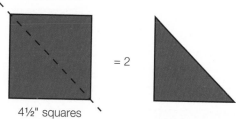 make 1	3" x 6" Directions are on page 29.
cut on diagonal	4½" sq.
Trim Border to:	6½" wide

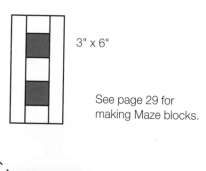

3" x 6"

See page 29 for making Maze blocks.

4½" squares   = 2

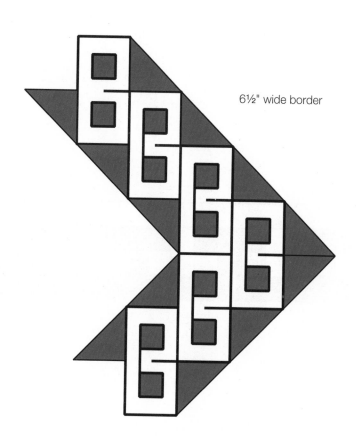

6½" wide border

Simple Border

Finished Border:		4"
cut 2		1½" sq.
☐ cut 2		1½" sq.
▬ cut 1		1½" x 2½"
☐ cut 1		1½" x 2½"
Trim Border to:		**4½"**

Sew:

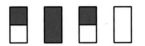 =   Repeat this block.

Add 1½" cut strips.

Add 1½" cut strips.

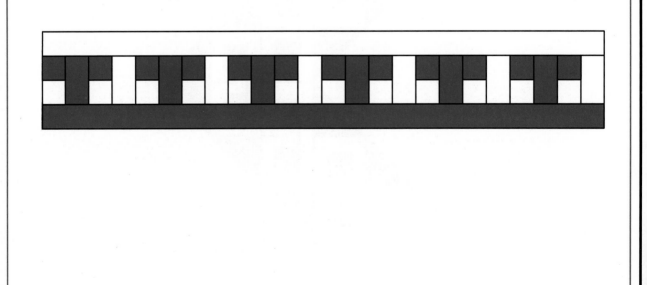

FOR ONE REPEAT

Finished Size	6" x 6"
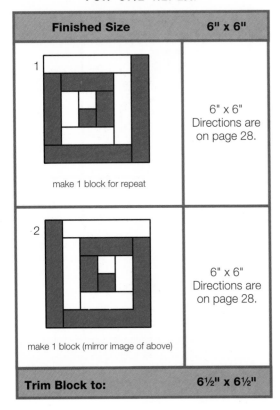 1 make 1 block for repeat	6" x 6" Directions are on page 28.
2 make 1 block (mirror image of above)	6" x 6" Directions are on page 28.
Trim Block to:	6½" x 6½"

Repeat 1 – 2 for border.

6" x 6" blocks

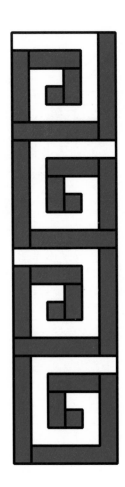

Use 5" x 5" blocks for a border.

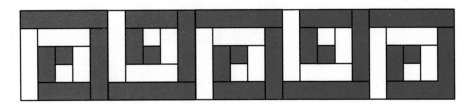

Balance inwardly and outwardly.

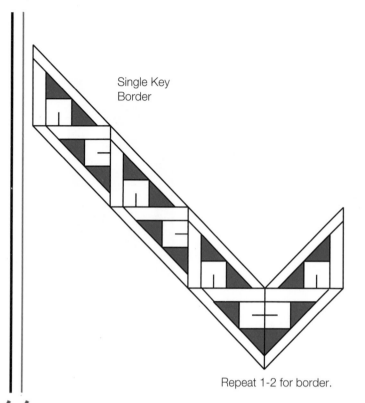

Single Key
Border

Repeat 1-2 for border.

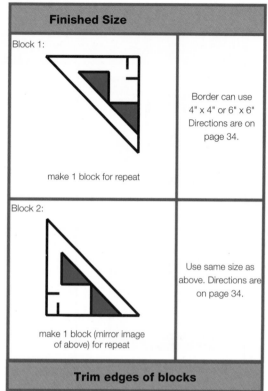

Finished Size

Block 1:	Border can use 4" x 4" or 6" x 6" Directions are on page 34.
make 1 block for repeat	
Block 2:	Use same size as above. Directions are on page 34.
make 1 block (mirror image of above) for repeat	

Trim edges of blocks

Double Key
Border

A wider Key border can be made by using double rows of the Key Blocks.

Half of the key blocks are
made mirror image.

Celtic Finishing Stitching

When a Celtic quilt top is complete, the top, batting, and backing are layered and safety pinned together. A zigzag stitch approximating a satin stitch is then applied to all the block-joining seams, outlining all the blocks. Zigzag detail lines are applied within the individual blocks, following Celtic design lines. By adding the zigzag stitching in place of most of the machine quilting, two steps are combined into one.

Black thread is my choice for stitching when I want to approximate the chiseled lines of the Celtic stonework or jewelry, or the inked lines of the Celtic manuscripts.

Gold or silver thread approximates the illuminated parts of the Celtic manuscripts. If dark fabrics are used the gold or silver thread is more effective. Because of the strength of Celtic designs, even gold and silver thread provides a subtle embellishment. In my quilts there are areas of black stitching or areas of silver or gold stitching; they have not been intermixed.

I was timid with my initial Celtic quilts and used a smaller zigzag stitch. Now I use a fairly wide zigzag stitch that emphasizes the bold designs. Experiment to find the right size of stitch until you feel comfortable with it.

An actual satin stitch is too invasive to the quilt and it creates too many needle holes in the quilt top. A satin stitch looks great up close, but the zigzag stitch gives the same effect from a distance, which is how most quilts are viewed.

The zigzag stitching joins the layers of the quilts, so little or no additional machine quilting is required. When you are applying your stitching, do not rely on memory; use a diagram in front of you as you stitch your quilt. The diagram should show the finishing Celtic design lines needed on the repeat blocks.

A wonderful bonus happens as you zigzag stitch your quilt; a Celtic design begins to grow on the back side. Give some thought to using plain or almost plain light fabric on the quilt back and a dark (usually black) bobbin thread to contrast with the quilt back fabric.

When you zigzag a Celtic quilt in silver and gold, use an off-white or light thread in the bobbin and a dark fabric for the quilt back.

If the black zigzag stitching skips occasionally, fill in the area with a dash from a permanent fabric pen.

I feel a deep connection to the Celtic scribes who inked in the same lines in the manuscripts that I make with my zigzag stitch. This realization makes my Celtic quiltmaking joyful meditation. As the quilt is turned from front to back and the design on the back grows, I feel a sense of bridging the past, and dream of creating the next link.

Celtic Crosses

Finished Quilt:	35" x 35"
cut 16	5½" sq.
make 24 blocks	5" x 5" Directions are on page 48.
make 1 block	15" x 15" Directions are on page 49.
Trim Center Block to:	15½" x15 ½"
Trim Remaining Squares to:	5½"x 5½"

68

CELTIC CROSSES (cont.)

35" x 35"

15" center block

5" blocks

35"

69

Project Designs

Celtic Repeat Panels – Woven Cord

Finished Panel	14" x 14"
make 4 blocks	7" x 7" Directions are on page 42.
Trim Blocks to:	**7½" x 7½"**

14" x 14"

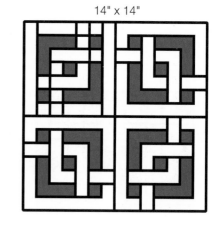

Celtic Repeat Panels – Key Blocks

Variation 1:

Finished Panel	9" x 9"
make 2	6" x 6" Directions are on page 34.
make 2	6" x 6" Directions are on page 34.
Trim Panel to:	**9½" x 9½"**

Sew: 9" x 9"

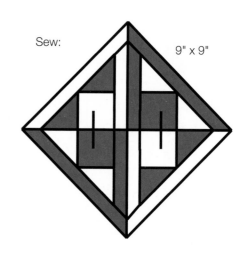

Variation 2:

Finished Panel	12" x 12"
make 4	6" x 6" Directions are on page 34.
make 4	6" x 6" Directions are on page 34.
Trim Panel to:	**12½" x 12½"**

12" x12"

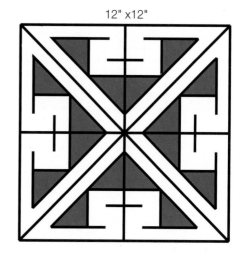

70

CELTIC REPEAT PANELS – KNOT BLOCKS

Finished Panel	24" x 24"
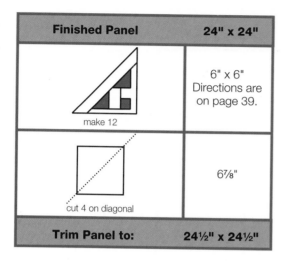 make 12	6" x 6" Directions are on page 39.
cut 4 on diagonal	6⅞"
Trim Panel to:	**24½" x 24½"**

24" x 24"

CELTIC REPEAT PANELS – MAZE & KEY BLOCKS

Finished Panel	18" x 18"
make 2 blocks and 2 reversing the color	6" x 6" Directions are on page 28.
make 4 blocks	6" x 6" Directions are on page 34.
make 4 blocks (mirror image of above)	6" x 6" Directions are on page 34.
Trim Panel to:	**18½" x 18½"**

18" x 18"

Celtic Repeat Panel – Maze, Fret, and center of Woven Cord Blocks

Finished Panel	21" x 21"
make 4 blocks	7" x 7" Directions are on page 21.
make 4 blocks	7" x 7" Directions are on page 28.
make 1 block	7" x 7" Directions are on page 42.
Trim Blocks to:	**7½" x 7½"**

21" x 21"

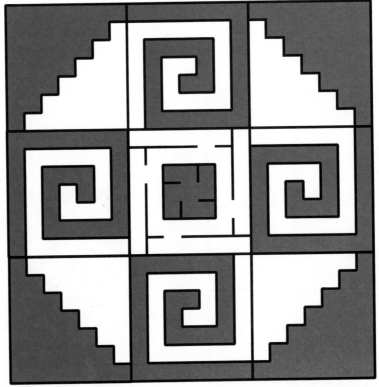

This could be made in 6" x 6" blocks for an 18" x 18" panel.

7" blocks

CELTIC STAR

Finished Quilt	24" x 24"
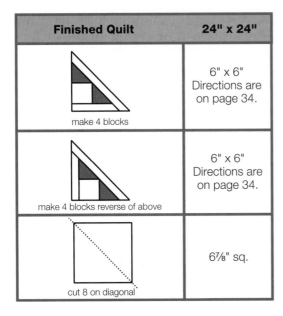 make 4 blocks	6" x 6" Directions are on page 34.
make 4 blocks reverse of above	6" x 6" Directions are on page 34.
cut 8 on diagonal	6⅞" sq.

For Center	
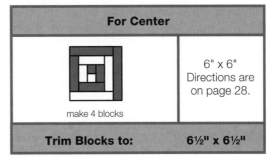 make 4 blocks	6" x 6" Directions are on page 28.
Trim Blocks to:	6½" x 6½"

24" x 24"

MAZE & KEY COMBINATION

Finished Size	26" x 34"	30" x 39" Shown
make 7 Maze blocks	6" x 6" Directions are on page 28.	7" x 7" Directions are on page 28.
make 17 blocks and 17 reverse	6" x 6" Directions are on page 34.	7" x 7" Directions are on page 36.

Celtic stitch center of quilt with silver
thread and the borders with black.

MINIATURE MAZE

Finished Size		18" x 24"	30" x 40"
make 24 Maze blocks		3" x 3" Directions are on page 30.	5" x 5" Directions are on page 30.
make 11 Key blocks		4" x 4" Directions are on page 34.	7" x 7" Directions are on page 36.
make 13 reverse Key blocks		4" x 4" Directions are on page 34.	7" x 7" Directions are on page 36.

DIAGONAL MAZE

Finished Panel	25" x 34"
make 20 blocks	3" x 3" Directions are on page 30.
make 10 blocks	6" x 6" Directions are on page 30.
cut 20 on diagonal	4⅞" sq.

Trim blocks with ¼" seeam allowances

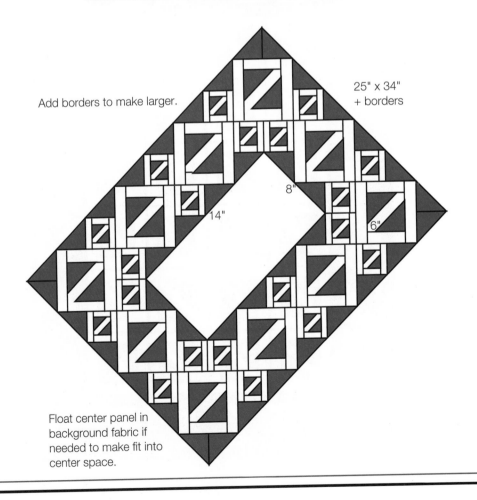

Add borders to make larger.

25" x 34" + borders

8"

14"

6"

Float center panel in background fabric if needed to make fit into center space.

ENDLESS KNOT

Finished Endless Knot Panel	11" x 14" with corners
Strips 1 & 1R	
cut 4	1½" x 3½"
cut 2	1½" x 2½"
cut 2	1½" sq.
Strips 2 & 2R	
cut 8	1½" sq.
cut 6	1½" sq.
cut 2	1½" x 3½"

Strip 3	
cut 3	1½" x 9½"
Strips 4 & 4R	
cut 2	1½" x 2½"
cut 8	1½" sq.
cut 6	1½" sq.
Triangles	
cut 2 on diagonal	7" sq. for corners

11" x 14" with corners
1 sq. = 1"

Sew: 1   2   3   4   3   4R   3   2R   1R

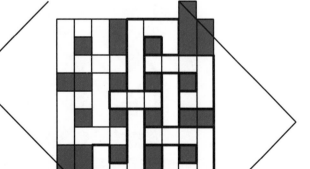

R = rotate 180 degrees

FOUR PATHS CROSSING

Center Block		
▭ cut 2	1½" x 7½"	
▭ cut 4	1½" x 5½"	
◼ cut 9	1½" sq.	
◻ cut 6	1½" sq.	

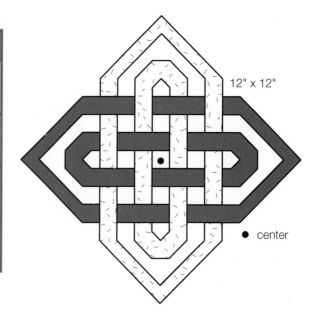

12" x 12"

● center

Step 1:

Sew center block.

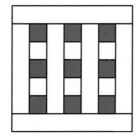

Trim to 7½" x 7½".

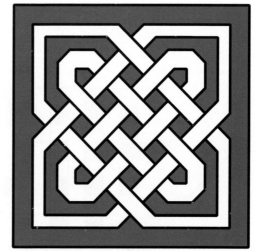

Finished panel on the diagonal.

FOUR PATHS CROSSING (CONT.)

4 Corner Sections	
cut 8	1½" x 2½"
cut 20	·1½" x 2½"
cut 9	1½" sq.
cut 8 for corners	1" sq.
cut 12	1½" sq.
cut 4 on diagonal	2⅞" sq.
	1½" strips to float panels

Step 2:

Make 4 corner sections.

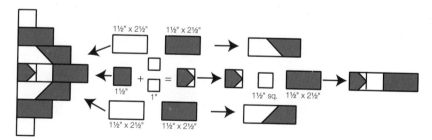

Trim corners sections and add cord strips.

Four Paths Crossing (Cont.)

Step 3:

Sew corner sections to center section.

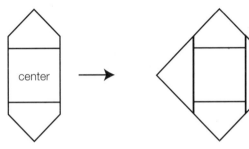

Step 4:

Cut away.

Cut away.

Cut 2½" sq. in half on diagonal.
Sew 2½" x 2½" triangles on each
end of 2 corner sections.

80

Repeat blocks for a quilt. Add borders and sashing strips to make quilt larger.

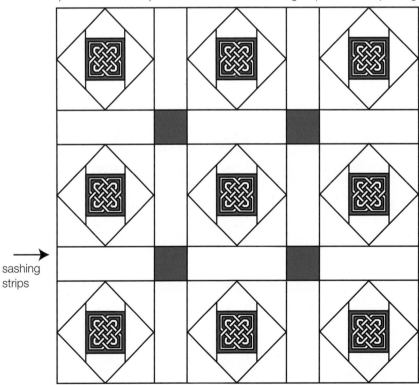

sashing
strips

THE GRAIL

Finished Quilt	36" x 40"
make 48 blocks	4" x 4" Directions are on page 30.
make 1 block and 1 mirror image	4" x 4" Directions are on page 21.
make 14 blocks	2" x 4" Directions are on page 29.
cut 2	4" sq.
cut 2 for corners	3" sq.

Borders	
make two strips for top and bottom borders	4½" x 28½" Directions are on page 55.
make two strips for side borders	4½" x 32½"

36" x 40"

THE GRAIL
58" x 68"

82

🌱 My second favorite quilt, The Grail, symbolizes the search for wisdom. This quilt, made of left-over blocks from the Excalibur quilt, demonstrates the flexibility of the repeat block technique.

THE GRAIL (BACK)

🌿 The back of this quilt is very effective on its own. The Celtic stitching lines provide depth and symbolic meaning for the designs.

LIFE IS COMPLEX

7" blocks   21" x 21"

For a more complex design, use many colors for the woven cords or many background shades.

1 sq. = 1"

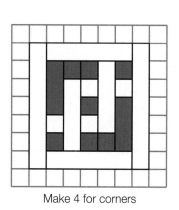

Make 4 for corners

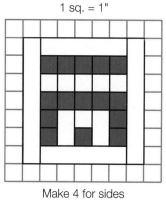

Make 4 for sides

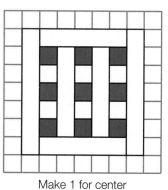

Make 1 for center

Note: If many colors are used, redraw the block diagrams for cutting and sewing.

LIVES ENTWINED – THE REPEAT BLOCK

Finished size:	6" x10"
Strip A	
cut 1	1½" x 2½"
cut 1	1½" x 2½"
Strip B	
cut 1	1½" sq.
cut 1	1½" sq.
cut 1	1½" x 3½"
Strip C	
cut 1	1½" x 3½"
cut 1	1½" x 5½"

Strip D	
cut 1	1½" x 3½"
cut 1	1½" x 5½"
Strip E	
cut 1	1½" sq.
cut 1	1½" sq.
cut 1	1½" x 3½"
Strip F	
cut 1	1½" x 2½"
cut 1	1½" x 2½"

❧ Two cords are entwined suggesting the complexity of life.

Two cord border

•ABC   See *ABC   See *DEF

Trim A   Trim

To make block: Sew •ABC + row 2, 3, 4, 5, 6 (Two Cord Border) + *DEF. Trim edge, leave a ¼" seam allowance. Add cut strips. Float block in background of cut 1½" strips.

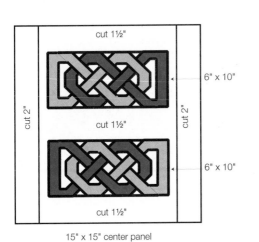

cut 1½"
cut 2"   6" x 10"   cut 2"
cut 1½"
6" x 10"
cut 1½"
15" x 15" center panel

8" x 12" center panel with 1½" cut floating strips.

Lives Entwined I

Finished Size		26" x 30"
make 14 Maze blocks		4" x 4" Directions are on page 30.
make 4 Maze blocks for corners		5" x 5" Directions are on page 30.
make 1 Lives Intwined repeat block		8" x 12" Directions are on page 91.
Borders		
make simple Celtic border		Top and bottom: 5" x 20" Side: 5" x 16" Directions are on page 55.

26" x 30"

26" x 30"

❦ These small wallhangings are quick to finish and will give you confidence in block construction. The two shown here were made for fund-raising projects.

LIVES ENTWINED II

Finished Size	33" x 37"
make 16 Maze blocks for corners	5" x 5" Directions are on page 30.
make 1 Lives Intwined repeat block for center	15" x 15" Directions are on page 91.
Borders:	
for top and bottom, make Double Hearts border	5" x 34" Directions are on page 55.
inner border, top and bottomcut two strips	1½" x 25½"
inner border, sides, cut two strips	2" x 27½"
center border, sides, cut two strips	1½" x 27½"
outer border, sides cut two strips	2" x 37½"

33" x 37"

87

31" x 37"

The Celtic designs on the back are formed by the use of the zigzag stitching on the blocks.

PLAYING WITH GREEN AND PURPLE

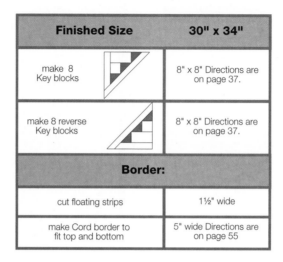

Finished Size	30" x 34"
make 8 Key blocks	8" x 8" Directions are on page 37.
make 8 reverse Key blocks	8" x 8" Directions are on page 37.
Border:	
cut floating strips	1½" wide
make Cord border to fit top and bottom	5" wide Directions are on page 55

Use lighter shades for the eight center Key
blocks and darker shades for the border.

30" x 34"

KNOT PANEL

Finished Size	10" x10"
cut 2	1½" x 5½"
cut 4	1½" x 3½"
cut 4	1½" x 2½"
cut 2	1½" x 3½"
cut 2	2½" x 5½"
cut 6	1½" sq.
cut 2	1½" x 6½"
cut 2	1½" sq.
cut 2	2½" sq.
cut 2	1½" x 2½"
cut 2	2½" x 3½"

Use in the four corners of a quilt.

Use as repeat blocks.

Sew:

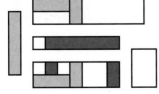

•Make 2 sections
•Turn 1 section 180 degrees and sew sections together matching centers.

5"   10" x 10"

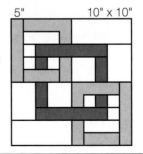

Celtic Jewel
42" x 54"

🌿 One key block has been repeated, using blue, green, and warm purple to create an attractive Celtic pattern. The stitching lines have been sewn in variegated silver thread.

CELTIC QUEST
68" x 80"

🌿 As is the case with all quests, this Celtic Quest quilt was the first step of my journey into Celtic quilts.

BIRDS ENTWINED IN A SQUARE

Finished Size approx. 9" x 10" strips	
cut 14	1½" sq.
cut 2	1½" x 2½"
cut 2	1½" sq.
cut 2	1½" x 2½"
cut 2	2½" x 3½"
cut 2	1½" sq.

cut 1	1½" x 3½"
cut 2	2½" x 3½"
cut 4	1½" sq.
cut 2	1½" x 2½"
cut 6	1½" x 3½"
cut 2	2½" x 3½"

1 sq = 1"
Approx. 9" x 10" +
floating strips

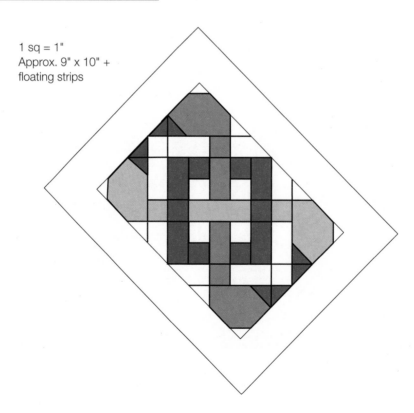

BIRDS ENTWINED IN A SQUARE (CONT.)

Sew:

Make center:

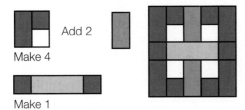

Add 2

Make 4

Make 1

Add to 4 sides:

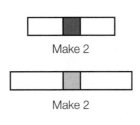

Make 2

Make 2

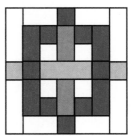

Make 2

Make 2

Trim away excess fabric.
Leave a ¼" seam allowance.
Add background strips.

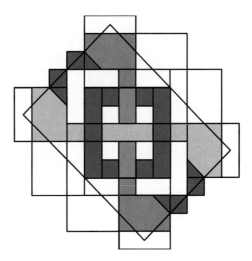

93

CELTIC BIRDS

CELTIC BIRDS
66" x 78"

94

Many Celtic drawings depict stylistic birds and animals. These birds are my only attempt to adapt this concept. The gold Celtic stitching on the borders provides light within the dark areas.

Excalibur — The Sword
68" x 74"

Excalibur is the name of King Arthur's sword, and represents just power. Two distinct color schemes have been used: yellow and purple, and red and blue. I have used black Celtic stitching in the light areas, and gold stitching in areas that benefit from highlighting.

EXCALIBUR – THE SWORD

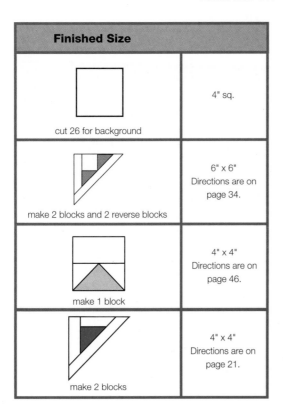

Finished Size		
cut 26 for background	4" sq.	
make 2 blocks and 2 reverse blocks	6" x 6" Directions are on page 34.	
make 1 block	4" x 4" Directions are on page 46.	
make 2 blocks	4" x 4" Directions are on page 21.	

make 1 block for handle. Cut two 1½" x 4½" strips to add a strip to each side	2" x 4" Directions are on page 29.	
make 18 blocks	4" x 4" Directions are on page 34.	
Borders		
cut two borders for top and bottom	6½" x 20½"	
cut two borders for sides	6½" x 28½"	

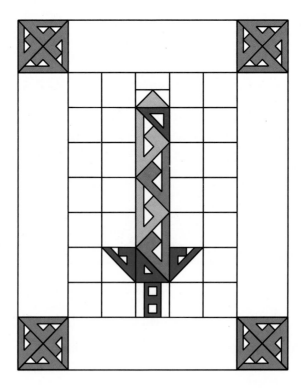

Borders – 4" – 6" wide
Corners – 16 – 4" x 4"

THE KEYS TO HAPPINESS

Finished Size	72" x 80"	
Center	make 24 blocks	4" x 4" See page 33 for making Fret blocks.
	make 48 blocks	4" x 4" See page 34 for making Key blocks.
Back	make 88 blocks	4" x 4" See page 32 for making Fret blocks.
Border:		
	make 68 blocks	8" x 8" See page 37 for making Key blocks.

Other Design Ideas
- Design a center section, 24" x 30"
- Use any 4" x 4" block, e.g. Maze.
- Use 1 or 2 cord borders and square corners.

Project Designs

Woven Knot Panel

Finished Size		9" x12½"
2 Colors	■ cut 17	1½" sq.
	▭ cut 12	1½" x 2½"
	from a 2½" strip, cut two	2½" sq.
	from a 2½" strip, cut two strips	2½" x 8½"
	from a 2½" strip, cut two strips	2½" x 13½"
3 Colors	■ cut 17	1½" sq.
	▨ cut 10	2½" sq.
Strip C	▭ cut 12	1½" x 2½"
	▦ cut 6	2½" x 4½"

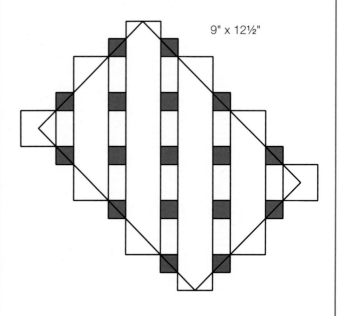

9" x 12½"

Celtic Stitching:

Optional – stitch in middle of wide strips.
Make larger if needed.

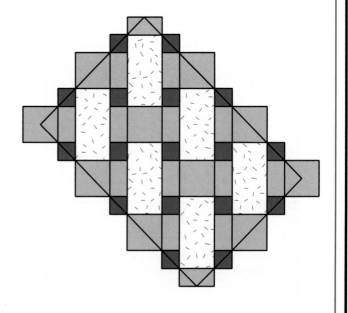

98

INITIAL POSSIBILITIES

"T" Block Quilt	45" x 45"
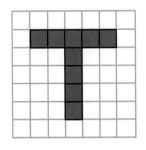 make 11 blocks	5" x 5" Use any Maze block see pages 27 – 31.
cut 26 for background	5½" sq.
make 2 Celtic Cross blocks, cut floating strips 1" wide for the sides and 2" wide for the top and bottom	10" x 15" Directions are on page 9.
make 2 blocks	7" x 7" Directions are on page 9.
cut 2 for filling in at corner	2½" x 3½"
cut 2 for filling in at corner	3½" x 5½"
Borders	
Make two strips for sides: (directions are on page 53)	**5½" x 30½"**
Make one strip for top:	**5½" x 31½"**
Make one strip for bottom:	**5½" x 35½"**

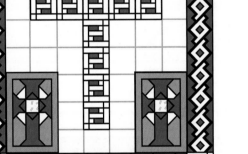

45" x 45"

"D" Block Quilt	35" x 45"
make 10 blocks	Select any 5" x 5" block from pages 16 – 18.
make 2 blocks	Select any 5" x 5" Key block from pages 16 – 18.
cut 23 for background	5½" sq.
cut 1 on diagonal	5⅞" sq.
Border	
make 44 blocks.	5" x 5" Directions are on page 34.
cut 8	5½" sq.

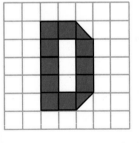

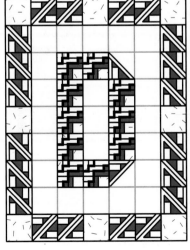

"P" Block Quilt	35" x 45"
■ cut 10	5½" sq.
□ cut 22	5½" sq.
◹ cut 2 on diagonal	5⅞" sq. for corner fill in blocks
Border	
◺ make 44 blocks	5" x 5" Directions are on page 34.
■ cut 8	5½" sq.

Using 6" x 6" blocks, quilt will be 42" x 54"

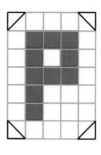

"J" Block Quilt	45" x 45"
◺ make 21 blocks	5" x 5" Directions are on page 34.
◹ cut 2 on diagonal	5⅞" sq. (3 triangles will be used).
□ cut 32	5½" sq. for background
make 1 symbol block, such as Grail for corner	10" x 10"
make 1 symbol block, such as Excalibur or Celtic Cross for corner	15" x 15"

"J" Block Quilt		35" x 45"
Make 2 blocks for corners.		5" x 5" Directions are on page 28.
Borders		
Make two strips for bottom and right side. Directions are on page 54.		**5½" x 25½"**
Make two strips for top and left side.		**5½" x 30½"**

Using 6" x 6" blocks, quilt will be 42" x 54"

45" x 45"

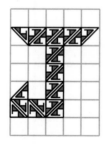

UNFINISHED QUEST

Finished Size		18" x 24"
center panel – using 1½" sq. and 1½" x 3½" strips		8" x 12"
make 22 Maze blocks		2" x 4" Directions are on page 29.
cut 8 on diagonal		3⅞" sq. for inside border fill-in
cut 14 on diagonal		3⅞" sq. for outer border fill-in

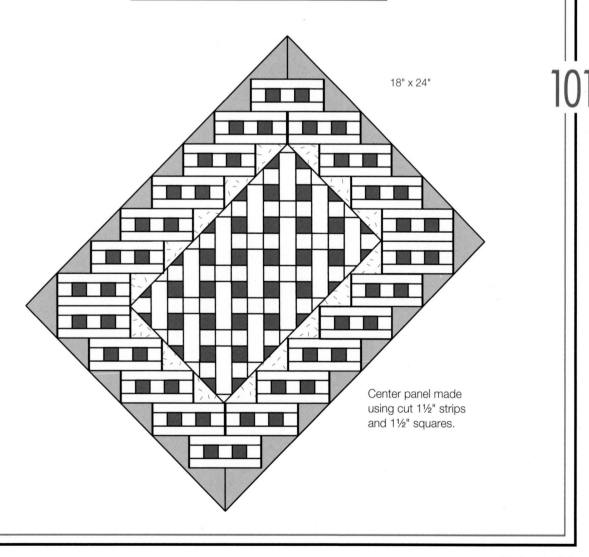

18" x 24"

Center panel made using cut 1½" strips and 1½" squares.

CONCLUSION

The making of many Celtic quilts over a two-year period became my Celtic journey. Although the journey, the quest, the search for meaning is an outward search in mythology, it is symbolic of the real journey, that of knowing oneself.

The quest is intended to awaken one to the inward journey. The search is really for self knowledge and self awareness. The ultimate answers – the real quest – lies within, not without. Will this always be an unfinished quest?

102

Bain, George. *Celtic Art: The Method of Construction.* London: Constable and Company Ltd., 1973.

Bain, Iain. *Celtic Key Patterns*. London: Constable and Company Ltd., 1993.

Davis, Courtney. *The Celtic Art Source Book*. London: Blandfort Press, 1988.

_____. *The Art of Celtia*. London: Blandford Press, 1993.

Fontana, David. *The Secret Language of Symbols*. San Francisco: Chronicle Books, 1994.

Lang, Lloyd and Jenneifer. *Art of Celts*. London: Thames and Hudson Inc., 1992.

103

ABOUT THE AUTHOR

Camille's love of sewing started as a child making doll clothes, continued as she made clothing for her family and decorated their home, and developed as the owner of a wool and crafts store. Deciding to make one quilt was the turning point that led to many changes in her life.

Her techniques and methods for quiltmaking are time-efficient and unique – she works only with cut strips, but the finished product captures the eye with amazing shapes and creative use of color.

From a business career (a B.S. in economics), Camille has shifted her main focus to the elements of design and creativity. *Celtic Geometric Quilts* is her sixth book in the last six years.

Camille, who resides in Ontario, Canada, teaches and lectures internationally.

AQS BOOKS ON QUILTS

This is only a partial listing of the books on quilts that are available from the American Quilter's Society. AQS books are known the world o their timely topics, clear writing, beautiful color photographs, and accurate illustrations and patterns. Most of the following books are availabl your local bookseller, quilt shop, or public library. If you are unable to locate certain titles in your area, you may order by mail from the AME QUILTER'S SOCIETY, P.O. Box 3290, Paducah, KY 42002-3290. Customers with Visa or MasterCard may phone in orders from 7:00–4:0 Monday–Friday, Toll Free 1-800-626-5420. Add $2.00 for postage for the first book ordered and $0.40 for each additional book. Include item n title, and price when ordering. Allow 14 to 21 days for delivery.